Published by Strawberry Reads Publishing, an imprint of Strawberry Publications, LLC
© Copyright 2016
First Printing 2016
ISBN 978-0692746776

This book is dedicated to the growing minds of our children.

123 COLORING BOOK

THIS BOOK BELONGS TO

_____

Strawberry Reads

Children's Books and Young Adult Publishing

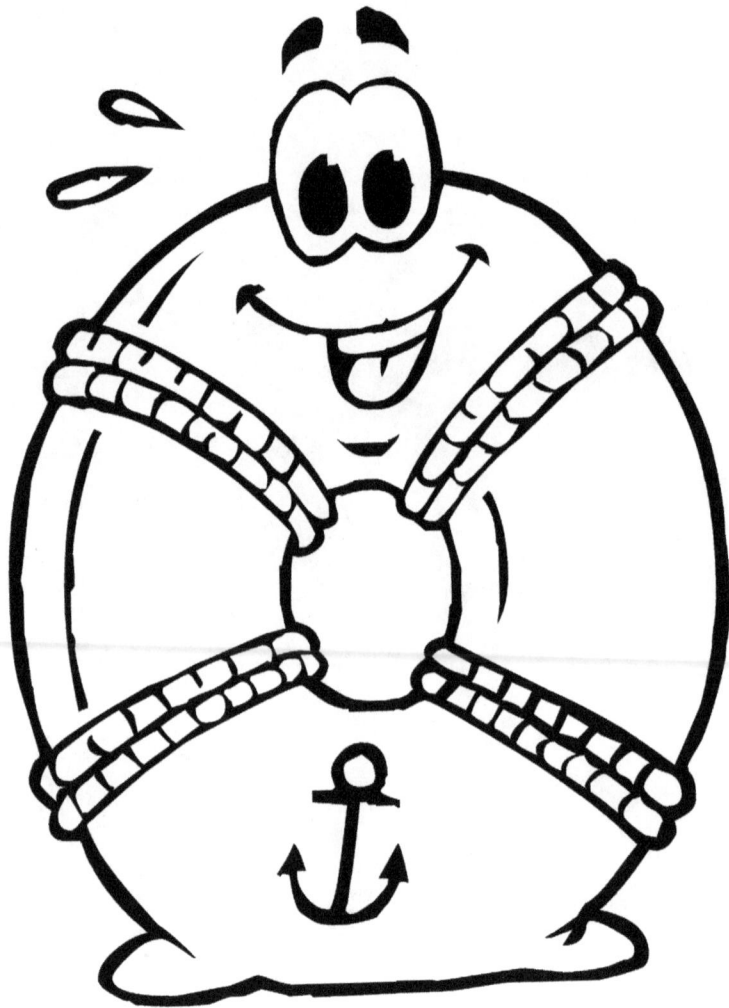

0

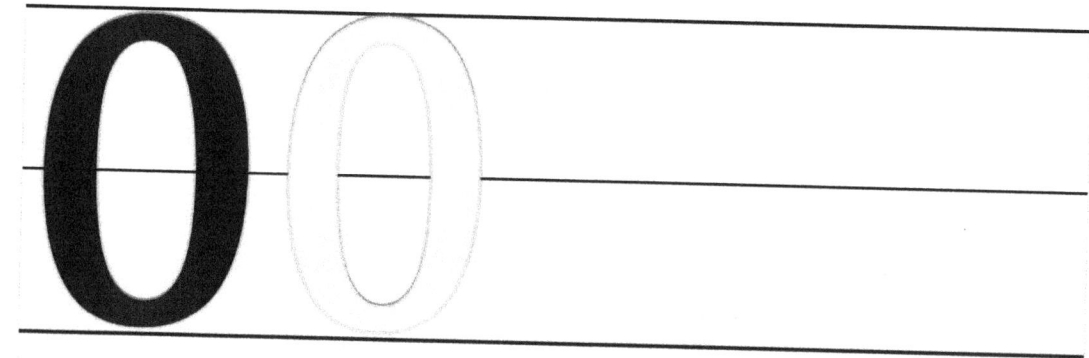

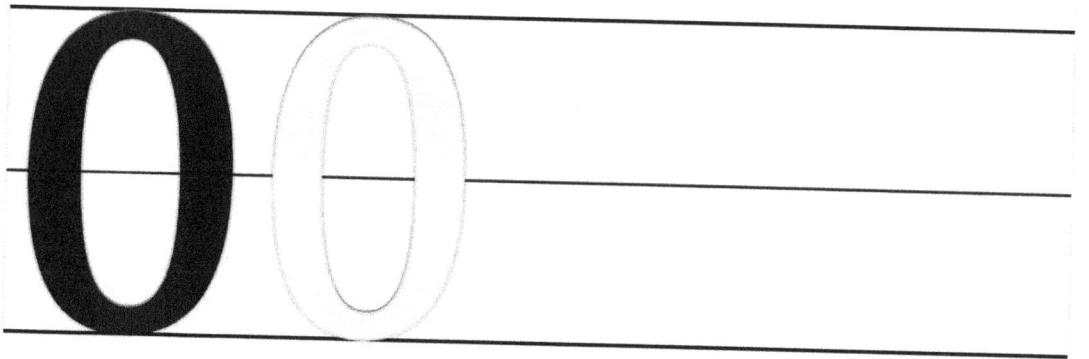

1

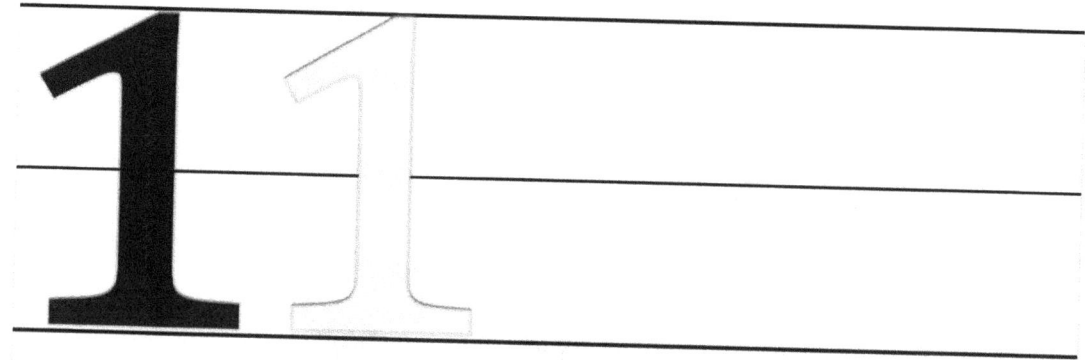

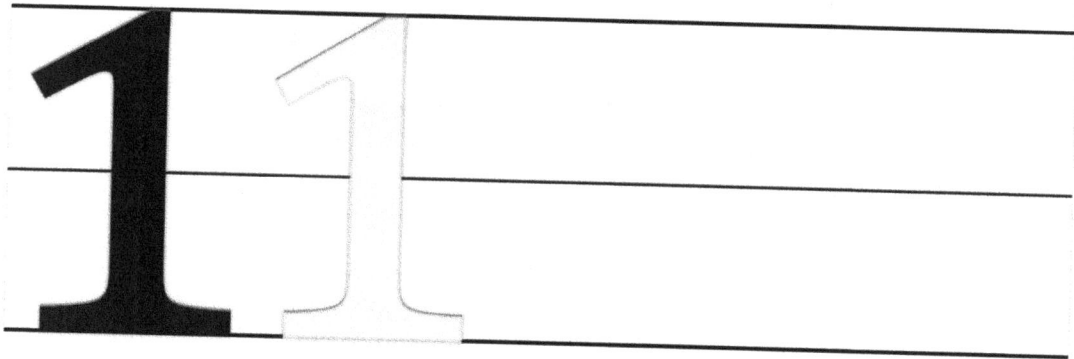

2

2 2

2 2

3

3 3

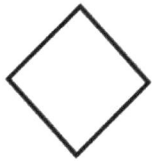 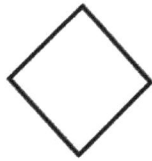 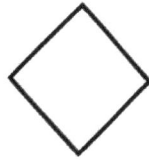

3 3

4

4 4

4 4

5

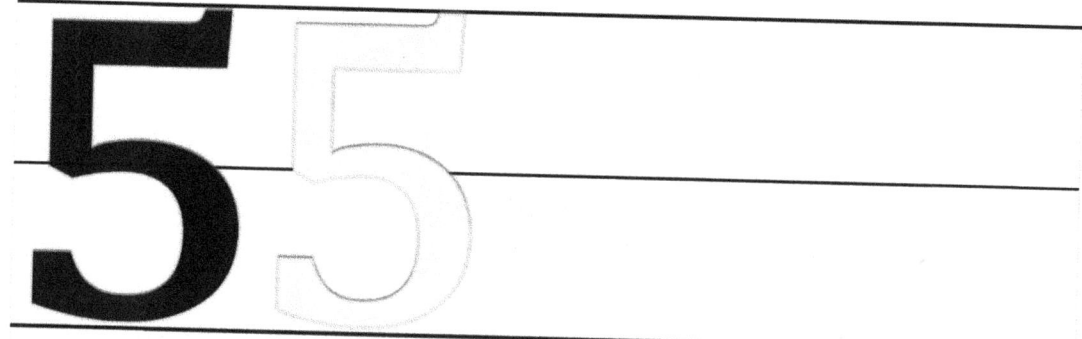

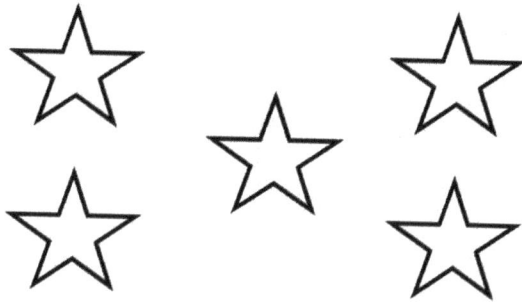

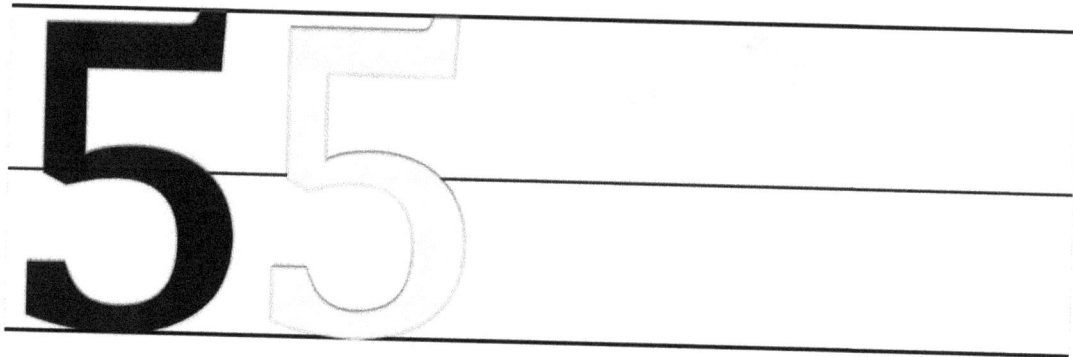

6

6 6

6 6

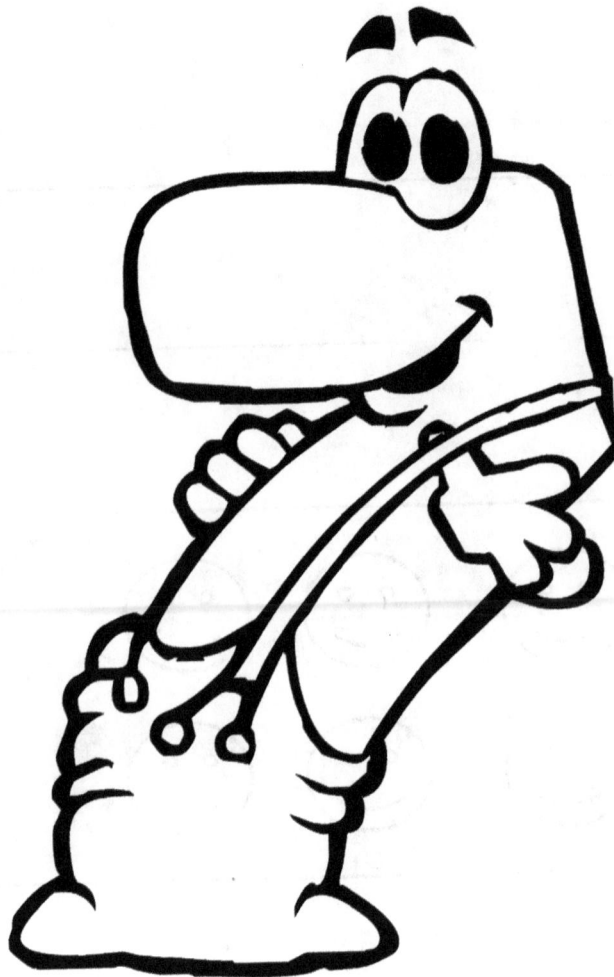

7

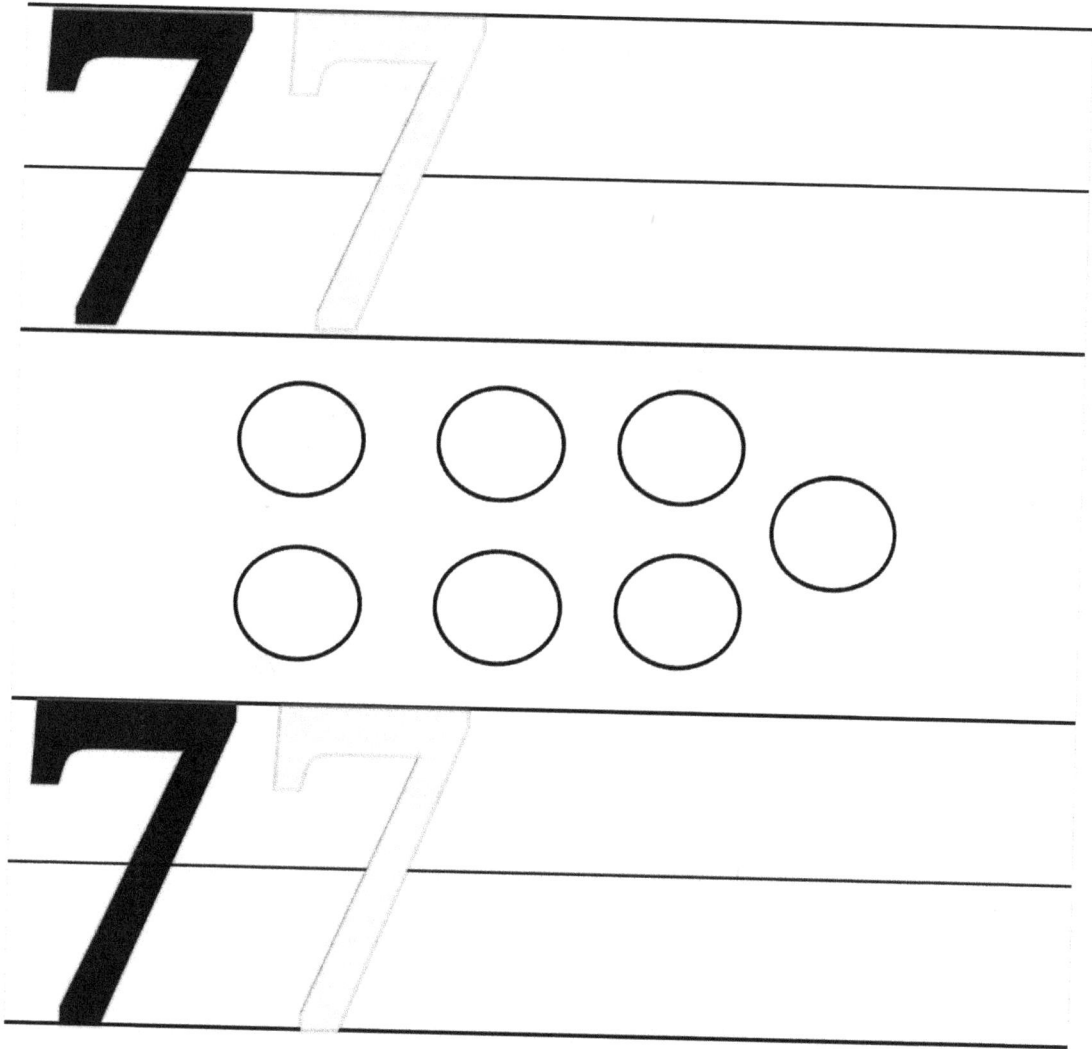

8

8 8

  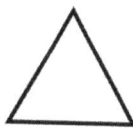 

8 8

9

9 9

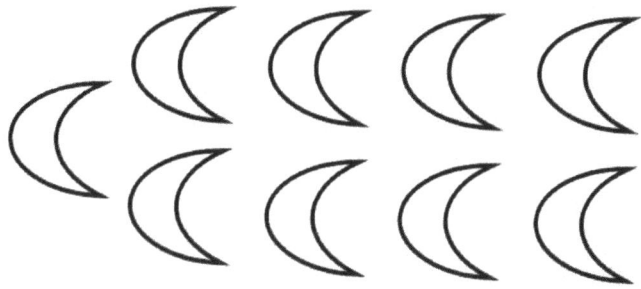

9 9

CONGRATULATIONS!!

www.ingramcontent.com/pod-product-compliance
Lightning Source LLC
Chambersburg PA
CBHW080537030426

42337CB00023B/4772